D1568276

# Jean Nicolet
## and the
# Sign of the Thunderbird

written by
Peter and Connie Roop

illustrated by
Lori McElrath-Eslick

River Road Publications, Inc.

Library of Congress Control Number: 2002094919


Jean Nicolet and the Sign of the Thunderbird
ISBN: 0-938682-74-1
Printed in the United States of America

Copyright © 2003  by River Road Publications, Inc.
Illustrations © 2003  by Lori McElrath-Eslick

# Contents

# *Prologue*

In 1634, Jean Nicolet, a French explorer, landed at Red Banks, Wisconsin, near the mouth of the Fox River. Red Banks had long been a home of the Ho-Chunk Indians, the first native people Nicolet met when he reached Wisconsin over 350 years ago.

This is the story of Moninga, a Ho-Chunk boy, and his first encounter with Jean Nicolet.

# Chapter One

"Come, Moninga. Sit at my fire,"
Nijunga said. "You have no father to prepare
you for your fast. I will tell you how a Ho-
Chunk boy seeks his Manitou." The old
warrior sat as always, running his hands
over the figure of the Thunderbird carved
into the handle of his canoe paddle. The
Thunderbird was the sign of Nijunga's clan.
Never once in all of his visits had Nijunga let
Moninga hold the handsome paddle.

Moninga drew close to the fire and
dropped  a birch stick on the embers. The
birch branch sputtered before yellow flames

leaped up, chasing the shadows to the far corners of the wigwam. Etched by age, Nijunga's face looked as creased as folded buckskin in the fire's glow.

"Like all boys-to-be-men you must set forth on your fast, Moninga. You must leave the village until Manitou, the Great One, comes to you and shows you the path your life will follow."

Moninga wiggled impatiently. He knew all this. What he wanted Nijunga to tell him was how he would recognize his Manitou. How would he know which trail to follow? Would he be a warrior feared by his enemies? Would he be a hunter known for skill with bow and arrow? Was he to be a medicine man helping those hurt or troubled by evil spirits? Did his life's path lead to his becoming a chief to guide his people?

A sharp glance from Nijunga forced Moninga to be still.

"Since you were captured from the Outagamies ten winters ago, you have not been adopted into a Ho-Chunk clan. Listen for your Manitou with head and heart. Only then will you learn which clan will welcome you."

Moninga already knew which clan he wished to join: the Bear Clan.

"After your fast we will no longer call you Moninga, He-Who-Hunts-About-The-Earth. Your hunting for a place among the Ho-Chunk will be over. You will gain a new name upon your return, a name from your clan."

Moninga smiled, knowing he would chose the great black bear for his name.

The flames from the branch Moninga had thrown on the fire began to die down. In the dim light the boy could see that Nijunga's eyes were half closed. Moninga stood, thinking he had been dismissed. Suddenly Nijunga opened his eyes wide and stared at him.

"You *will* know your Manitou" Nijunga said. Then the old medicine man just as suddenly closed his eyes and was silent.

Moninga lifted the deer skin from the lodge entrance and stepped out into the cool night. He paused, looking around the Ho-Chunk village as if he were seeing it for the first time. The moon, as white as weathered limestone, shone above the Red Cliffs east of the village. Spread before him in a circle were the dome-shaped wigwams.

Although it was late, the village was not silent. A baby cried, its mother hushing it in a gentle voice. A dog barked, then yelped as its master threw a stick at it. The wind rustled the yellow tassels of the tall corn in the surrounding fields. Moninga could hear the slish slish slish of the waters of the bay lapping against the shore. All of this was familiar yet somehow strange after Nijunga's words.

Moninga looked west toward the main lodge of the Bear Clan, wondering whether his life's trail would lead through its doorway. Then Moninga, He-Who-Hunts-About-

The-Earth, went to the wigwam of Ahutco, his Ho-Chunk mother.

# Chapter Two

Moninga placed his bow and arrows, deer robe, and stone knife in the canoe. Before kneeling on the bottom of the birch bark craft he slipped on dry moccasins. The shadows of the gray dawn were broken as he dipped his paddle into the still water. Soon he would be far from the familiar village.

Moninga had purposely left before the morning fires were stirred. Yet he was still disappointed when no one came to see him set forth on his fast. No wise chief from the Thunderbird Clan. No brave hunter from the Clan of the Wolves. No fierce warrior from the Bear clan. Even Nijunga did not come. Moninga had never before felt so lonely, not even after he was captured from the Outagamies.

Keeping close to the shore, Moninga paddled north. It was the Corn Tassel Moon when the western winds could swoop across the bay and dash any unwary traveler against the cliffs. A flock of geese honked as they arrowed south. Moninga wished to raise his bow, bring down a goose, and feast upon its fat flesh. But he knew no food could pass his lips until his Manitou had appeared.

The day passed quietly. When he was thirsty, Moninga dipped his hands into the bay's clear water. When tired, he lay flat, listening as the restless water rocked his canoe.

As the sun dropped low on the western waters, Moninga steered to a sheltered cove. Lifting the small, light canoe, he carried it to a sandy spot at the forest's edge. He tilted the canoe on its side and crawled beneath it, pulling his deerskin robe over himself to keep the chill night air away.

His stomach growled. Moninga ignored the rumbles. He knew he could outlast them but it would be difficult to fast for three, four, maybe five days. He hoped his Manitou would appear early. Then, tired from his long day of paddling, he slipped into sleep.

All night dreams drifted through Moninga's head: dreams of his village, dreams of a great brown bear, dreams of a solitary canoe on a wide, windy water. The last dream remained with Moninga when he awoke and he wondered if his Manitou had appeared. All that day Moninga kept a sharp lookout for the canoe of his dreams. But he was alone on the lake.

Late that afternoon he paddled into a wide bay below steep cliffs towering above the inlet. At the foot of the cliffs lay a jumbled cobblestone beach. Leaning over the bay's calm waters was a single willow, barely anchored in the rocks. Moninga guided the

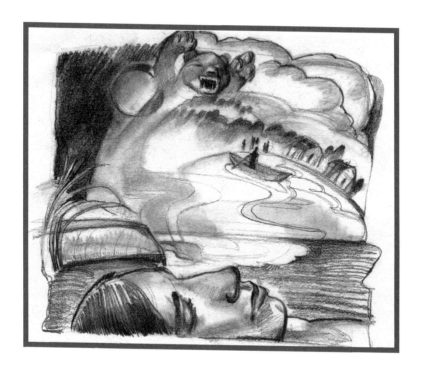

canoe beneath the drooping willow branches.
A horde of gnats, irritated by his intrusion,
swarmed around his head. He brushed them
away and landed. Moninga pulled his canoe
far under the protective branches hoping it
would be safe there.

Taking his robe, his bow and arrows, and
his knife, Moninga crossed the rocky beach

to the cliffs. As he walked along the foot of the cliffs he searched for a way to the top. Spotting a promising route, Moninga climbed, being careful not to uproot plants or dislodge rocks. He left no trace of his passage.

At the top, Moninga stopped to catch his breath. Green Bay spread before him, rippled by the wind. A great bald eagle soared above him. It circled the sky, searching for prey. As Moninga watched, the eagle dove to the water and snatched a fish with his deadly talons. The mighty bird lifted the wiggling fish and flew north along the cliffs. Moninga's stomach rumbled as he thought about the fine meal the eagle would devour. The sign of the eagle is a good omen, Moninga thought. He is powerful, he hunts, and other animals fear him.

Moninga turned from the cliff's edge to look for a site to build his fasting lodge. Not far back from the cliff he found a shallow stream coursing through a pine thicket.

Birches ringed a nearby meadow. Moninga decided to build his lodge close to the stream. Lying down, he dug his heels into the soft needles of the forest floor. He stretched his arms back over his head, scratching more marks into the soil. With these holes as guides, he made a circle. This would be his lodge circle.

Using his stone knife, Moninga cut a dozen saplings. After he sharpened both ends, he stuck the sticks into the ground, bending them one over the other to make a wigwam frame. He cut wide strips of bark from the birch trees and placed them over the frame. He carefully aligned the lodge entrance to the east to welcome Grandmother Sun each new day. At last he propped dead logs and large branches against the birch bark to hold it in place. Stepping back, Moninga looked at his fasting lodge. It might not weather a severe storm, but it would keep him dry in a shower.

He gathered rounded stones from the

creek and arranged them in a circle in the center of his lodge. Using brown birch twigs and pine needles as tinder, he soon had a fire glowing. Moninga wished he had a rabbit to roast or a slice of venison to sizzle over his fire. He would even welcome a bowl of steaming corn meal mush. His stomach grumbled.

Moninga went to the stream to drink to drown the rumbles. After drinking his fill at the stream he decided to walk to the cliff's edge to watch the sun slip away. As Moninga walked through the woods to the cliff the last light of the sun angled through the trees in bright yellow shafts as straight as spears.

"Grandmother Sun," he called out from the cliff's edge. "Give me strength to endure my fast. Give me your warmth to fill the chill of my empty stomach." As he prayed the sun disappeared behind the land across the bay. Moninga felt even lonelier than when he had left his village.

Back at his lodge, Moninga crushed

some charcoal from his fire, mixed it with water, and smeared his face black. Knowing he was following the traditions of the fast made him feel better. Manitou would surely speak to him now that his face was blackened the Ho-Chunk way.

Moninga lay down in his fasting wigwam, rustling the leaves he had scattered for his bed. Through the open door of the lodge he searched the autumn sky, his eyes sliding from star to star. His stomach rumbled like distant thunder.

Moninga rose and returned to the stream. He knelt in the soft sand, cupping his hands, and filling them with cool water. He knew he should drink silently like a true Ho-Chunk yet he slurped. On the opposite bank a raccoon raised its head to stare at him. He held a fish in his paws.

Moninga laughed. "Dark-eyed One. Eat all you want. I won't steal it from you. But after my Manitou appears, beware. I will know my trail and it just might cross yours!"

The raccoon returned to his fish.

Moninga raised his face to the rising moon, now bone-white above the enclosing trees. "Grandfather Moon," he said softly. "Think me not unworthy. I am hungry but only my stomach growls. My heart is still strong. I will fast until my Manitou comes."

A burst of wind, gusting through the trees, sprinkled leaves onto the stream. Moninga watched the rippling water catch the leaves, spin them, and carry them away. Moninga imagined them to be canoes drifting downstream towards some wonder-filled adventure. When the last leaf swirled away, Moninga returned to his fasting lodge. With a nod to Grandfather Moon, he went inside and lay down. Closing his eyes, he listened to the wind and the stream. Then Moninga sprinkled an offering of tobacco onto the fire. The sweet smell of the burning tobacco wafted through the wigwam as Moninga prayed that his Manitou would come that night.

During the night dreams flocked through Moninga's head like the geese which fill the autumn skies. He dreamt of Ahutco, his Ho-Chunk mother. He dreamt of wise Nijunga. He dreamt of a great eagle capturing a fish.

# Chapter Three

In the morning Moninga explored the forest surrounding his lodge. Following the stream, he found the tracks of a buck cut deep into the mud. He searched for the eagle's nest, hoping to find it and shoot the eagle for its feathers. Wouldn't Ahutco and Nijunga be proud of him if he returned with a clan Manitou as well as eagle feathers to decorate his hair?

Near the end of his walk Moninga felt dizzy. His head spun like a log in a whirlpool. He sat down on a rock, breathing as heavily as if he had run around his village three times. Gradually the dizziness disappeared, leaving in its place a lightheadedness that made Moninga feel as if he were part of a dream himself. His stomach grumbled, but Moninga ignored it. He stood and carefully walked back to his lodge. His only thought was for sleep. Maybe if he slept his Manitou would soon come.

Moninga smeared more charcoal on his face, dropped tobacco onto the fire, and prayed, "Spirits, am I likely to be blessed today? That is why I am praying." Then he pulled the deerskin robe over his shoulders and fell into an uneasy sleep. Moninga tossed and turned. His robe slipped off. Chilled, he awoke, pulled it back up, and dozed off again. His dreams focused on food: bear meat sizzling on a stick, sturgeon stewing, ducks dripping fat into a fire.

The warmth of Grandmother Sun shining on his face awoke him. He was hungry, but not as hungry as yesterday. Maybe my dream food filled my stomach, he thought as he went to get a drink of water. The chill of the cold water hurt his empty stomach, but he drank several times before returning to his hut for his bow and arrows.

"I will track my deer today," he said out loud. "If I find him and slay him, then I will have food when I end my fast."

Moninga did not roam far from his lodge. He had no energy. He wanted to hunt the deer, but he could not force his legs to carry him more than a few steps at a time. He returned to the lodge before the sun was directly overhead.

Moninga fell asleep in front of his lodge. This time no dreams drifted through his mind. He slept soundly and for a long time. When he awoke the afternoon shadows were stretched long across the meadow. Rubbing the sleep from his eyes, Moninga walked to the cliff. He stood gazing at the bay. His companion, the eagle, circled in the sky, hunting for fish.

Suddenly the eagle began to fall. One of

its widespread wings was bent back. A sharp
crack of thunder snapped in the crisp air. The
crackling echo rolled along the cliff. Moninga
watched wonderingly as the bird dropped
into the woods near the cliff's top. Never
before had he seen an eagle fall from the sky,
an eagle killed by thunder. Puzzled, Moninga
looked at the sky. No clouds darkened the
solid blue. Yet he knew he had heard a crack
of thunder.

25

Manitou! he thought. My Manitou has appeared!

The thought gave Moninga the energy he needed to run. Dodging rocks and trees he raced to the place where the eagle had fallen. He searched frantically for the bird. The eagle and Moninga saw each other at the same moment. The impressive bird, flapping its injured wing, glared viciously. Moninga walked slowly toward the struggling eagle. Seeing that a leg was broken, Moninga knew he must kill the eagle to end its misery.

"Brother Eagle," he said gently. "May your spirit always soar the skies."

Avoiding the sharp, flashing talons, Moninga stepped closer to the eagle. Drawing his knife, he waited for his chance and when it came, slashed the bird's throat. The eagle twitched twice before death claimed its spirit.

Moninga carried the eagle to his lodge where he carefully plucked the tail and wing feathers. He cut a large square from his robe to make a pouch to protect the feathers. All the while he puzzled over the bird's mysteriously broken wing and the thunder from the cloudless sky. He knew the eagle was his Manitou, but what did it mean? He had wanted to join the Bear Clan. An eagle had nothing to do with the Bear Clan.

When he lay down that night Moninga thought of the morning. Now that his Manitou had appeared he could hunt the deer and break his fast. Knowing this, he quickly fell asleep.

A stick snapped. Moninga opened his eyes and sat up, suddenly alert. Maybe the deer had wandered near his lodge. Inhaling silently he waited. Another crunch came moments later. Moninga reached across his lodge for his bow, and bent it back, fastening the drawstring tightly. Motionless, he waited for another sound before taking up an arrow.

Moninga strained to hear the deer breathing. The early morning birds welcomed the sun's return. The stream whis-

27

pered over its rocky bed. Notching an arrow, Moninga slipped to the lodge entrance.

If Manitou had spoken he surely would not miss the deer. He could break his fast, feasting on the deer meat before returning home in triumph to his village. In one swift movement Moninga raised the bow and jumped around the edge of the lodge. Pulling the string back he aimed. A squirrel, startled by his sudden movement, leapt to an oak, scolding Moninga as he dashed to safety.

The boy stifled the anger rising inside him. His hungry body had played a trick. What Ho-Chunk warrior would ever be fooled by a nut-hunting squirrel? Moninga reached back into the lodge and grabbed his quiver of arrows. Now he would hunt the real deer.

Moninga entered the forest. He set each foot down carefully, rolling from heel to toe so as not to make a sound. He moved toward the place where he had seen the deer tracks before and searched the dew-wet grass for deer signs. He snatched in his breath when he saw the deer nibbling grass at the far side of the meadow. Kneeling, he reached for an arrow. Then he stopped, openmouthed.

Across the field a man stepped from the morning shadows. The man raised a long stick and pointed it at the deer. The buck, aware and wary, lifted his head and looked at Moninga. The Ho-Chunk boy's eyes met the deer's eyes and an unspoken message passed between them.

The buck bent his head down to graze.

A crack of thunder split the forest still-ness. Smoke swirled around the man. The deer leapt into the air and fell to the ground. Slowly the cloud of smoke drifted from the man. The deer lay where it had fallen. Moninga stopped breathing as the man turned, his eyes searching the surrounding forest. The man's face, although covered with thick, black hair, was white!

Moninga watched him cross the meadow to the deer. He set his thunder-stick on the ground and pulled a knife from his belt. The knife was unlike any other that Moninga had ever seen. The blade flashed in the sun like a sharp chip of ice. The man with the skin of snow plunged the knife into the deer's haunch and carved away a leg. The blade sliced through the hide as easily as a canoe slices through water. He did the same for the other leg. Wiping the blade on the deer's hide, he stood and shouldered the deer's legs. Picking up his thunder-stick, the man retraced his steps across the meadow.

Moninga knelt as still as a stump the entire time, wondering if he was dreaming, Was this another sign from Manitou?

Long after the man had disappeared into the forest shadows Moninga went cautiously to the deer. The image of the eagle returned to him as he walked. A man with pale skin, a deer dead without an arrow, an eagle dropping from the sky.

Moninga took his own stone knife and cut out the deer's still warm heart, eating it in great bites. He sliced a thick piece of meat from the deer's side and hastened back to his lodge. He stirred the coals of his fire and roasted the venison.

Moninga could not remember venison tasting this good. He finished the meat, licked the fat from his fingers, and went to the stream for a drink. Kneeling by the stream, he cupped his hands full of the chilly water. As he lifted his hands to his mouth he bent his head back. His arms stopped halfway.

Staring at him from the other side of the stream was the white-faced man.

# Chapter Four

The man's eyes seemed to cast a net over
Moninga, holding him like a trapped duck.
The icy water trickled down Moninga's arms
and he shivered as he knelt by the stream.
But Moninga held the man's gaze and
choked down his fear.

Two Indian warriors stepped out of the
forest and joined the white man. Moninga
did not recognize them. He knew they were
not Ho-Chunk from the quill patterns on
their moccasins. Moninga kept this eyes on
the men as he slowly stood. He reached for
his knife at his waist then realized he had left

it in his lodge. He was unarmed.

The man with skin like snow raised his right hand in the sign of peace. His Indian companions did the same. Moninga answered, holding his open palms before him as if offering a present. The bearded man smiled but Moninga kept his face stiff.

The three men crossed to Moninga's side of the creek. Moninga's breath swished out of him suddenly. He had held it since the men appeared. The white-skinned man began talking slowly in a language Moninga could not understand. "Nic-o-lay," the white man said, tapping his chest. "Nic-o-lay," he repeated, holding his palms open in imitation of Moninga's sign of peace.

"Nic-o-lay," Moninga said, pointing to the man.

Nicolet pointed at Moninga.

"Moninga," the Ho-Chunk boy said.

Nicolet repeated, "Moninga."

Moninga stepped back. Now he recognized the quill patterns on the Indian moccasins. They were Hurons, enemies of the Ho-Chunks! One brave moved toward Moninga. The boy reached for his missing knife. Instead of harming him, the Huron warrior signed peace to Moninga and the boy relaxed. He felt that even if the Huron wanted to harm him, this strange Nicolet would protect him.

Turning toward the forest, Nicolet motioned for Moninga to follow him. The boy looked at the Huron warriors and stepped into Nicolet's footprints in the wet sand. Moninga glanced back at his wigwam and wished he had his knife. If he escaped, he would need his weapon. He longed for the eagle feathers Manitou had given him.

Moninga wondered if he was a prisoner of this man with the thunder-stick. Where were they taking him? They were moving towards the bay. Maybe they had found his canoe! If they had, he had no chance of escape. To reach his village through the bogs, swamps, and cliffs bordering the lake would take many suns. And he was half starved.

Moninga's frustration rose. He wanted to tell Nicolet he was a Ho-Chunk warrior. He wanted to say that if any harm came to him he would be revenged by the fierce fighters of his tribe. Yet the man's talk was strange to his ears. How could Moninga make Nicolet understand the power of his people?

The three men and the boy moved quickly and quietly along a deer trail down a broken slope of the cliff. At the bottom the trail curved close to the high limestone bluffs, skirting the bogs and hollows filled with stagnant water.

Once Moninga almost broke away to escape back up the rough ridge to his lodge. He dared to look at the Huron behind him. Even in the forest shadows Moninga could read the man's eyes. He knew Moninga was thinking of escape and he was prepared to stop him.

The bluffs turned sharply toward the

lake. Sunlight sparkled off the water like rock crystals. Within moments they reached the shore and walked down a cobblestone beach. This was the beach where he had hidden his canoe. He chanced a glance toward the willow  tree, hoping his Huron guard would not notice.

Moninga could not see any trace of his canoe. If his canoe was untouched, he was certain he could escape when night came. He would make his way to his people to warn them of the coming of the man with the stick of thunder.

Moninga's heart sank when he saw five more Huron warriors gathered around a campfire at the far end of the beach. His chances of escape drifted away like smoke in the wind.

The smell of roasting meat reached Moninga. Despite the danger, he thought of his stomach. Even the hint of food made his mouth water. Moninga's stomach rumbled so loudly Nicolet turned and looked at him.

Nicolet made an eating motion with his hands. Moninga recognized his offer. He imitated Nicolet's motions. Nicolet called to a Huron to bring the boy some deer meat.

The meat was hot and burned Moninga's fingers. He tossed it back and forth until it cooled enough for him to bite off a chunk. The juice ran down his face, making tracks in the charcoal on his chin.

When he had finished, Moninga pantomimed washing his face.

Nicolet understood and pointed to the lake. Moninga walked to the water to wash off the charcoal. His fast was over, his Manitou had given him a sign and he no longer needed the sacred charcoal on his face.

At the water's edge he peered down the shore at the leaning willow tree. He glimpsed the end of the canoe. Moninga glanced back. Nicolet was talking with the Huron leader. They pointed at Moninga and down the coast to the land of the Ho-Chunks.

When Moninga returned, Nicolet came to him. He spoke to the boy in the tongue of the Hurons. Moninga recognized only one word: Ho-Chunk. He was surprised this white man knew of his people. The gentleness of Nicolet's voice and the clearness of his eyes forced Moninga to put away his fears of this unusual man. There was something in Nicolet's eyes that made Moninga want to trust him. If only he could understand what the white man was saying.

Moninga could tell Nicolet knew he didn't understand his words. Signaling to the Huron leader, Nicolet spoke rapidly, pointing to the top of the cliff. The Huron motioned for Moninga to follow him.

Nicolet was sending him to be killed!

Moninga sprinted down the beach. He hoped to catch the Hurons by surprise and reach his canoe. As he ran he prayed to his Manitou. He heard the Hurons give cry and chase him. Dodging rocks and driftwood, Moninga dashed down the jagged shore. He didn't dare look back until he was an arrow's shot from the willow tree. Glancing over his shoulder he saw a Huron just behind him.

The man reached out and grabbed Moninga just as he touched the boughs of the willow. Their momentum carried them through the drooping branches. They tumbled in a heap onto the beach. Moninga swung at the Huron with all of his strength. But the man was too strong and he quickly pinned Moninga's flailing arms.

The man smiled when he saw Moninga's canoe.

Just then Nicolet pushed the branches aside and spoke to the Huron, who reluctantly released the boy. The warrior pointed at the canoe and Nicolet's face grew puzzled. He looked at Moninga, then at the canoe. Nicolet pointed at the canoe and at Moninga. The boy tried not to let his eyes reveal to Nicolet he was right, the canoe was his. Nicolet smiled and motioned for Moninga to come to him.

When Moninga  hesitated, the Huron pushed him. Ordering  the Huron to bring the canoe, Nicolet took Moninga with him toward the high bluff. Moninga was confused. Was Nicolet going to kill him? Where could he run this time?

At the edge of the beach Nicolet paused and looked at Moninga before starting up the path. Moninga decided he would not run again. He would go bravely to his death, showing Nicolet the bravery of a Ho-Chunk warrior. Grasping saplings and rocks, Nicolet made his way to the top of the embankment. He did not look back even once as he climbed. Moninga followed silently.

Out of breath when they reached the top, the man and boy looked over the bay. The big water spread beneath them ablaze with the sun's light. Hungry gulls careened and dove. A sentinel crow cawed a warning to his tribe that man was near. Nicolet gestured toward two wooden poles Moninga had not seen before. A striped blanket, strings of rainbow-colored beads, and an iron ax hung on the poles. They were a sign to tell all people that the bringers of such wealth brought friendship and peace.

Moninga's shoulders relaxed and he sighed when he saw the poles. He now knew Nicolet had indeed come in peace. He also understood his trail and this strange white man's trail had crossed. Manitou was showing Moninga his life's path.

Before they returned to camp, Moninga took Nicolet to his fasting lodge. Picking up his pouch of eagle feathers, Moninga opened it and showed the feathers to Nicolet. Nicolet pantomimed holding his thunder-stick at the sky. Moninga understood—Nicolet's thunder-stick had brought down the eagle. Nicolet was a Manitou, too. A Manitourinou, a Wonderful Man.

Moninga gave Nicolet the longest and straightest feather. Nicolet slipped the eagle feather into his hair, letting it fall gently down his back. Moninga did the same. Then

the Frenchman and the Ho-Chunk boy returned to camp.

# Chapter Five

In the morning Nicolet led Moninga to his canoe. At first, Moninga did not understand. Then Nicolet put his hand on Moninga's shoulder, pointing with his other down the shore. The white man made the sign of many people. He signed that he, Nicolet, would go to the many people. He pointed at Moninga, then at his canoe. Moninga understood. He was to return to his people and tell them Nicolet was coming to their village.

Nicolet pointed to himself, made the sign of peace, and signed many people again.

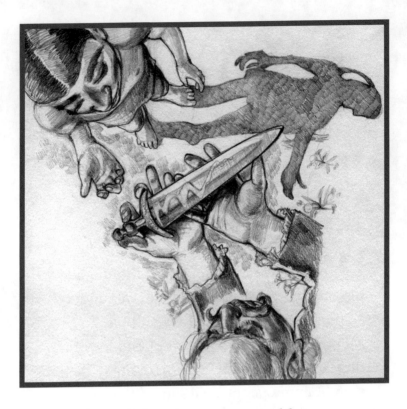

He indicated that three suns would pass
before he came. Then Nicolet reached for the
knife hanging from his belt and handed it,
handle first, to Moninga. Moninga turned the
knife over and over. Testing the blade's
sharpness, Moninga ran a finger down its
edge. A thin trickle of blood lined his finger.

Nicolet took the sheath from his belt and gave it to Moninga. Slipping the sharp blade into the sheath, Moninga turned and walked to his canoe. After pushing off, Moninga looked back and waved his paddle. Then with firm, steady strokes he began paddling to his people.

Moninga kept close to shore, knowing the dangers of being caught by a surprise storm offshore. It would take a day and half of the next for him to reach his people. He paddled all morning without stopping. When his arms ached he reminded himself of the news he was bearing.

Noticing the sun had reached its highest point, Moninga decided to rest. He ate some of the meat the Huron leader had placed in his canoe before he left and drank from the lake. He checked the pouch of eagle feathers to make sure they were still safe and dry. Moninga let the canoe drift as he rested and thought about all that had happened since he left his village to fast. His Manitou had appeared. He was no longer a boy in the eyes his people. He was now a man. He could join the Bear Clan. He had met a mysterious white man who held thunder and death in his hands and was not harmed by them. And now, he Moninga, was a messenger to tell his people of the coming of Manitourinou.

When he reached the Ho-Chunk village at Red Banks, Moninga went to Nijunga's wigwam. Seeing no trace of charcoal on Moninga's face, Nijunga knew the boy's fasting had been successful. He also noticed the eagle feather in Moninga's black hair. Without a word Nijunga stirred his fire and placed a clay pot of corn near the coals.

Sitting down opposite Nijunga, Moninga lay the leather sheath with the steel knife between them. Nijunga still did not say a word. Moninga was a man now, an equal in the tribe, and Nijunga must wait for him to speak first. Moninga could hardly contain his excitement. He wanted to blurt out his story. The words welled up inside like spring melt water building behind a beaver dam. He knew once he began, he would not be able to stop until all of the words had flowed freely away.

Nijunga removed the pot from the coals. He set the steaming bowl beside the knife sheath and indicated that Moninga eat. Moninga dipped his fingers into the hot mush, savoring the corn meal. He ate as much as was polite, then stopped, and offered the bowl to Nijunga. While Nijunga ate, Moninga settled on the best way to tell his story. He would tell first of Manitou, then of the man with the snow-white skin. He would tell of Nicolet's coming to Red Banks last. When Nijunga was finished he looked at Moninga and nodded.

Moninga told his tale, "I went north two suns to the white cliffs. There I built my fasting lodge and covered my face with charcoal. I burned the sacred tobacco and prayed to the spirits. For three suns no food passed my mouth. All day and night I listened for Manitou, for the Great One's words to tell me the path of my life. For three days and nights not a word. But on the fourth day an eagle fell from the sky. I heard thunder but saw no clouds. I found the eagle and took its fine feathers."

Moninga took the feathers from the pouch, handing them one by one to Nijunga. The medicine man rubbed his bent fingers over the feathers. "The eagle is my Manitou," continued Moninga. "I was not sure until the next morning when I met a man with skin like snow. He killed a deer with a stick of thunder. With that same stick he had killed the eagle."

Moninga paused, seeing that Nijunga did not understand what he meant by stick of thunder. "This man, Nicolet he calls himself, holds thunder in a long, hard stick. He makes fire burn in this stick. A powerful medicine kills whatever this stick is aimed at.

"Nicolet had with him seven Huron warriors and they took me to their camp."

Nijunga tensed at the mention of the Hurons, but Moninga explained, "They meant me no harm although at first I thought they would send my spirit away from my body. Nicolet comes in peace."

Moninga stopped and dramatically pulled the steel knife from it sheath. "He gave me this medicine knife as proof of his friendship." Moninga handed the knife to Nijunga. The polished steel reflected the orange glow from the fire and Moninga saw amazement on the old man's face. Nijunga turned the blade over and over in wonder, running his hand along the handle and lightly touching the blade.

Nijunga spoke for the first time. "Nicolet," he said, slowly turning the word over. "I have heard of strange men with white skin. Now Moninga has seen one. He tells me this man holds thunder and death in his hands yet comes in peace. He travels with seven Huron warriors and speaks their tongue. Nicolet is a Manitourinou."

Warmth spread through Moninga, a warmth like sunshine after a fierce rain shower. Nijunga had called Nicolet Manitourinou, just as he had. Handing the knife back to Moninga, Nijunga stood and said, "Moninga, come with me. We must tell the tribe of this. We must send Ho-Chunk warriors to meet Manitourinou."

Moninga and Nijunga went to the lodge of Xora Hunga, Bald Eagle Chief. Nijunga spoke quietly with Xora Hunga. The Ho-Chunk chief sent Moninga to bring the other leaders to his lodge. When the men had gathered, Nijunga told them of the Moninga's news. All wished to hold the strong medicine knife. Then they talked. Two logs burned through as the leaders debated Moninga's news. Some wanted to move the village so that Nicolet could not find them. Others wanted to attack and kill him and the treacherous Hurons.

Moninga remained silent while the men talked. He was surprised when Xora Hunga

asked," Moninga, what do you think?"
Moninga had never before spoken at a council meeting. Boys were not allowed to speak at such gatherings. Moninga remembered that since his Manitou had spoken to him he was no longer a boy, he was now a true Ho-Chunk adult.

Moninga hesitated. He had been listening to the different arguments and had not made up his mind about them. First he had agreed with those who said move away. Then he had agreed with those who said fight. But as he remembered Nicolet's eyes and the moment at the top of the cliff he knew what he had to say.

"We must meet Manitourinou." Moninga's voice grew firm as he spoke. "He brings us peace with the Hurons and peace with his people. He also brings us medicine knives, thunder-sticks, cooking pots which never break, beads of all the colors of the rainbow. I will stay and meet him. Those who wish the same may join me."

With these words Moninga stood up. Alone. The older Ho-Chunks looked at the boy-turned-man. One by one they stood until the entire council was on its feet.

"We must send a party to greet Nicolet when he reaches our people," Nijunga said. "Let Moninga lead three warriors to greet Nicolet."

The council agreed.

"But first," continued Nijunga, "Moninga must join the Clan of the Thunderbird, the clan of peace as well as war."

Xora Hunga, Bald Eagle Chief, asked, "What name do you choose to be called as you enter the Clan of the Thunderbird?"

Moninga was caught off guard. He had hoped to join the Bear Clan. Now he was asked to the Thunderbirds, the clan of the chiefs. "May I wait, Xora Hunga, to join the clan? I have no name chosen."

Xora Hunga agreed to Moninga's request. "Yet you will enjoy the rights of the

Thunderbird Clan until you have chosen your new name. Carry this symbol of your clan." Xora Hunga gave Moninga a soft buckskin upon which was drawn two rainbow arrows, the sign of the Thunderbird.

# Chapter Six

Moninga and his three companions left at dawn to meet Nicolet. They paddled their two small canoes half the morning before spotting the large canoe bearing the French- man and his Huron friends. Nicolet greeted Moninga when the boy's canoe pulled up alongside his own. Moninga swelled with pride as his Ho-Chunk brothers saw the friendliness which Nicolet showed him. Turning their canoes, the Ho-Chunks led Nicolet to Red Banks.

Even when they were far from shore, Moninga could see the entire encampment had gathered to greet Nicolet. With strong, steady strokes he urged his companions to paddle in unison. While most eyes would certainly be on the big canoe carrying Nicolet, some eyes would be on Moninga's. He wanted to reach shore first so he would be ready to greet Nicolet when he reached the beach.

Moninga jumped out of the canoe the moment it touched land, leaving his partner to pull the boat onto the beach. Moninga rushed to where Nicolet would land and reached the spot just as the long birch bark canoe ran up on the sand. The Ho-Chunks pulled back leaving a wide strip of beach between themselves and Nicolet.

Moninga had been so intent upon being the first to reach shore that he had not noticed the unusual clothes Nicolet wore. Like his fellow tribesmen, Moninga now stared at the long flowing robe covered with brilliantly colored flowers and flying birds. Trimmed with gold as yellow as the sun, the

blue robe was more beautiful than a summer sky.

Moninga moved back as Nicolet stepped onto the beach, raised two small thunder-sticks and fired them. The boom of the pistols startled everyone. Women and children fled to the protection of the forest. The echo of the shots bounced off the cliffs. When their sound died away there was an empty silence.

Moninga recovered from his surprise and walked up to Nicolet, opening his hands in the peace sign. Nicolet handed his fire sticks to Moninga and opened his hands, too. Then Xora Hunga stepped forward, opening his right hand in friendship. Nicolet walked up the beach with his Huron companions following. One unfurled a large French flag. The wind caught the flag, snapping it back and forth.

Everyone began talking at once: Nicolet, the Hurons, the Ho-Chunks. Although the words weren't understood, each party knew the other offered friendship. Feeling a hand on his arm, Moninga turned to see who it was. Tcega, who had once been a captive of the Hurons, pulled him away from the crowd. Moninga followed him reluctantly.

"Moninga," Tcega said, "it has been many seasons since I lived with the Hurons. Yet as I heard these men speaking, much of their tongue came back to me. My voice is too feeble to shout above the crowd. Tell

Xora Hunga I can translate their words so we may all understand why they have come to the land of the Ho-Chunks."

Moninga squeezed through the crowd to Xora Hunga and repeated what Tcega had said. Raising his voice, Xora Hunga quieted the crowd. "Tcega, come forward," he called. Everyone waited silently as the old man came up to the chief.

The elderly Ho-Chunk had once been a brave warrior. Respect showed in his people's faces as he addressed Nicolet. "What land do you come from, Man-With-The-Snow-Skin? Why do you come to the country of the Ho-Chunk?"

"I come from a land far across a great water," Nicolet replied. "My chief, Champlain, sent me to make peace between the Huron and their Ho-Chunk brothers."

Tcega turned to the Ho-Chunks and repeated Nicolet's words.

Xora Hunga stepped forward to Nicolet, offering the highest symbol of peace, tobacco. Nicolet took the tobacco and presented Xora Hunga with a steel knife. A murmur went up from the crowd, followed by a shout. Moninga was pleased. He knew his people were accepting Nicolet and the Hurons.

News of Nicolet's arrival spread rapidly to the many villages scattered along the shores of Green Bay and the Fox River. During Nicolet's visit hundreds of Indians came to see this Manitourinou with hands of thunder. The people feasted and ate many beaver tails in honor of Nicolet.

One day Nicolet approached Moninga. Tcega was with him to translate his words.

"Moninga," Nicolet began. "In ten suns I will leave my friends the Ho-Chunks to travel up the Fox River to continue making peace with the tribes there. It is likely I will be gone through the winter. There will be many dangers. I would like you, Moninga, to come with me as a Ho-Chunk warrior."

For a moment Moninga could not find

the words to reply. He had wanted Nicolet to winter with the Ho-Chunks so he could learn his language and see more of the wonders which Manitourinou possessed. Most of all, Moninga wanted to make thunder with Nicolet's pistols. Now Nicolet wanted Moninga to join him in his travels!

"I must ask Nijunga," Moninga finally answered.

"I hope he agrees, my friend," Nicolet said.

Moninga entered Nijunga's lodge where Nijunga sat holding his Thunderbird paddle.

"What it is?" Nijunga asked after Moninga had seated himself by the fire.

"Nicolet has asked me to go with him," Moninga said. "He will not return this winter to his people as he wishes to journey up the Fox to make peace there. I am seeking your advice, Grandfather."

Nijunga said nothing for a long while. He kept his eyes on the paddle. At last he spoke. "Moninga. I have given much thought about the coming of the white men to our lands. There will be changes, good changes and bad. You were the first of our tribe to meet a white man. Your trails are crossed. Listen to your Manitou. You are a Ho-Chunk brave now and must make this decision yourself."

"But Grandfather," Moninga said. He wanted permission to travel with Nicolet, not to have to make his own choice.

Nijunga ignored his protest and instead handed him the Thunderbird paddle. Stroking the broad blade Moninga thought of his fast, of the eagle, of meeting Nicolet. He knew what his choice would be.

"I will go with Nicolet," Moninga answered. "I will learn more of his ways and return to my people to share them."

"Those are the words of a Ho-Chunk of the Thunderbird Clan. Those are the words of a chief."

When the day came for their departure, Moninga helped the Hurons pack the large canoe. Then he said farewell to Nijunga and Ahutco and joined Nicolet on the beach. The beach was not empty like the morning he left on his fasting journey. Today every Ho-Chunk in the village was there.

Moninga took his place in the canoe, clutching his paddle. They pushed off and backed away from shore. Nicolet tapped Moninga on the shoulder. He held out a thunder-stick. Moninga stood and, in view of all his people, held the thunder-stick aloft. The powder exploded as he pulled the trigger. He knew now what name he would choose upon his return: Konihega, He-Who-Thunders. Konihega of the Thunderbird Clan, a chief of the Ho-Chunk. Moninga could still hear the echo of the pistol shot as he dug his Thunderbird blade into the clear water. That echo remained with Konihega the rest of his life.

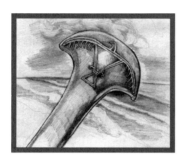

# About the Authors

Peter and Connie Roop have written more than 60 children's books. Their books have been recognized by the National Association of Science Teachers, National Council of Teachers of English, the Children's Book Council, and the American Library Association.

Peter, a Wisconsin State Teacher of the year, has written extensively for *Cricket* and *Cobblestone* magazines. He now writes and speaks full time.

Connie, a high school environmental science teacher, is a recipient of the Women Leaders in Education Award from the American Association of University Women and a Kohl Education Foundation Award for Exceptional Teaching.

# About the Illustrator

Lori McElrath-Eslick grew up in rural Michigan, which fostered her interest in the landscape. She often paints on location for her own enjoyment. Lori has illustrated many children's books, including *Da Wei's Treasure*, *Mommy Poem*, *Nishnawbe*, and *Hen and Chick*.